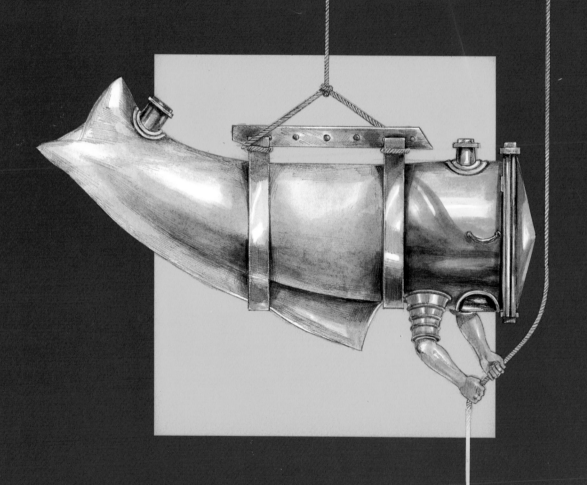

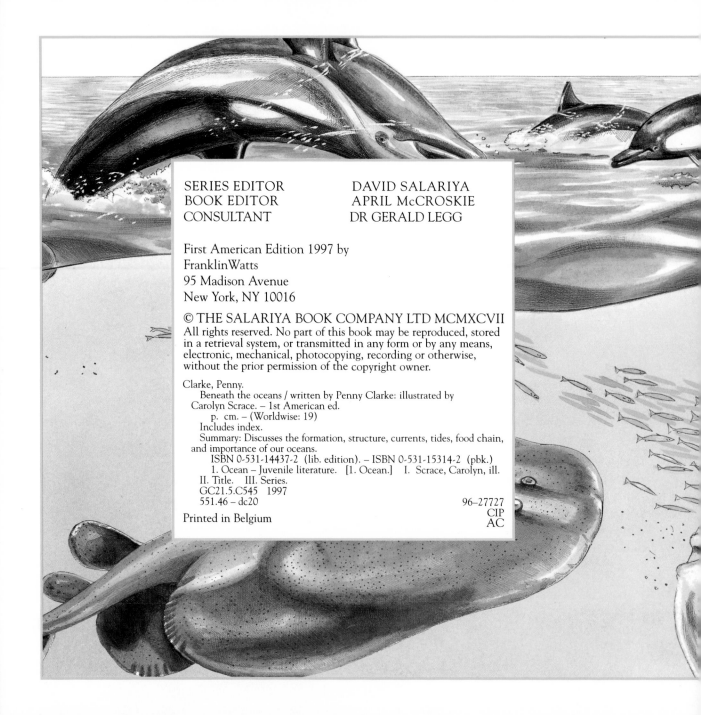

SERIES EDITOR   DAVID SALARIYA
BOOK EDITOR   APRIL McCROSKIE
CONSULTANT   DR GERALD LEGG

First American Edition 1997 by
FranklinWatts
95 Madison Avenue
New York, NY 10016

Clarke, Penny.
   Beneath the oceans / written by Penny Clarke: illustrated by
Carolyn Scrace. – 1st American ed.
     p. cm. – (Worldwise: 19)
   Includes index.
   Summary: Discusses the formation, structure, currents, tides, food chain,
and importance of our oceans.
     ISBN 0-531-14437-2 (lib. edition). – ISBN 0-531-15314-2 (pbk.)
     1. Ocean – Juvenile literature. [1. Ocean.] I. Scrace, Carolyn, ill.
II. Title.   III. Series.
GC21.5.C545 1997
551.46 – dc20   96–27727
                                       CIP
                                       AC
Printed in Belgium

beneath
the oceans

Written by
PENNY CLARKE

Illustrated by
CAROLYN SCRACE

Series Created & Designed by
DAVID SALARIYA

FRANKLIN WATTS
A Division of Grolier Publishing
New York•London•Hong Kong
Sydney•Danbury, Connecticut

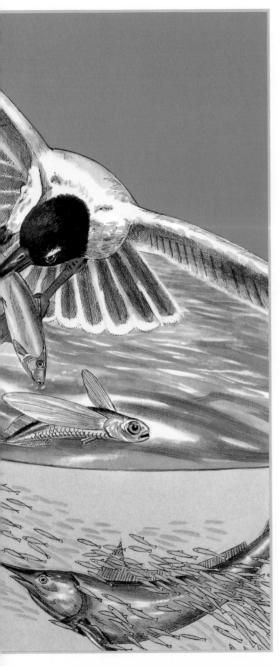

Oceans are large basins in Earth's surface that contain salt water.

Today they cover over 70 percent of Earth. Seas are similar but smaller. If these basins were dry there would be no life on Earth, because scientists believe that life developed in the oceans and moved onto land much later.

Where did the water in the oceans originally come from? No one can be sure, but today much of it comes from deep within Earth. When the volcanoes on the ocean bed erupt, they pour out water from far beneath the oceans.

About 220 million years ago Earth had just one vast ocean and one huge landmass. Then, about 100 million years ago, the landmass began to crack and the ocean water surged in. This was the beginning of today's continents and oceans. The process continues. An ocean is forming between Africa and Arabia as the land slowly drifts apart.

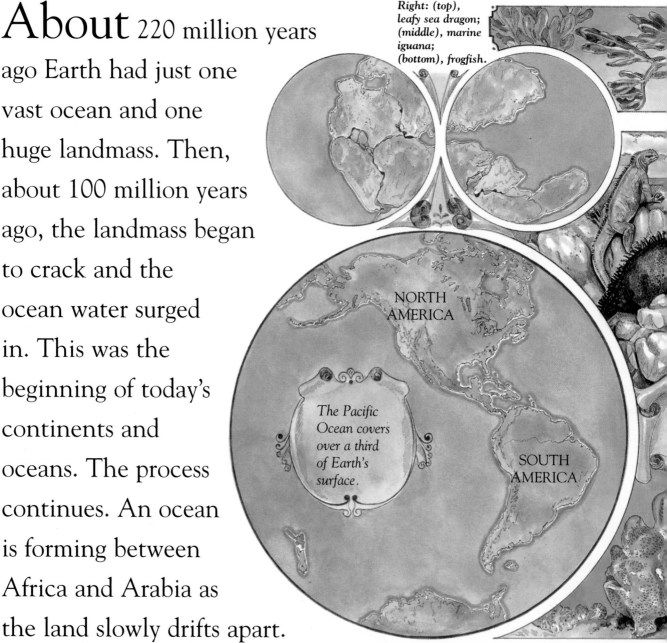

Right: (top), leafy sea dragon; (middle), marine iguana; (bottom), frogfish.

NORTH AMERICA

The Pacific Ocean covers over a third of Earth's surface.

SOUTH AMERICA

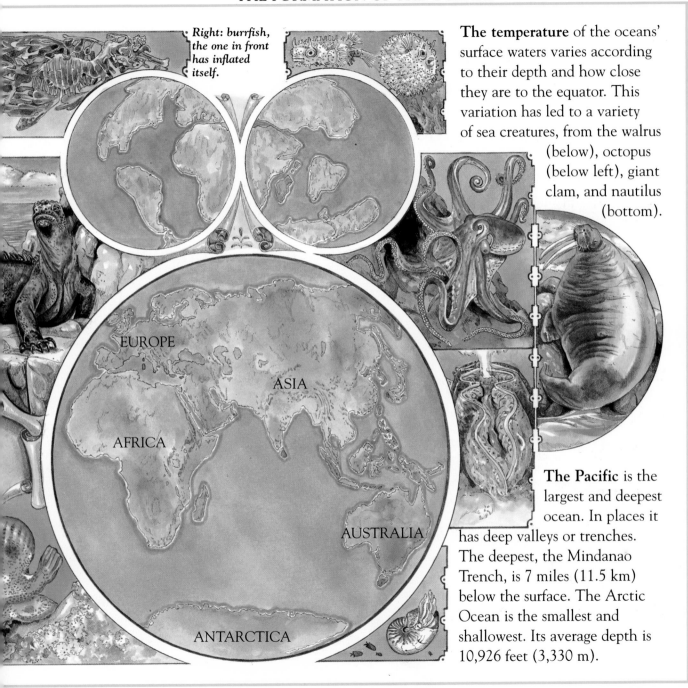

Right: burrfish, the one in front has inflated itself.

EUROPE

ASIA

AFRICA

AUSTRALIA

ANTARCTICA

The temperature of the oceans' surface waters varies according to their depth and how close they are to the equator. This variation has led to a variety of sea creatures, from the walrus (below), octopus (below left), giant clam, and nautilus (bottom).

The Pacific is the largest and deepest ocean. In places it has deep valleys or trenches. The deepest, the Mindanao Trench, is 7 miles (11.5 km) below the surface. The Arctic Ocean is the smallest and shallowest. Its average depth is 10,926 feet (3,330 m).

The pressure of Earth's movements makes rocks buckle and bend. So the strata (layers) in which rock forms are seldom straight.

Scientists believe that the first huge continent split because of movements of Earth's crust below the ocean. Much of the deep ocean floor is flat, but there are also mountain ranges. Pressure from deep within Earth forces the ocean bed away from the ranges and molten rock surfaces to form a new ocean bed.

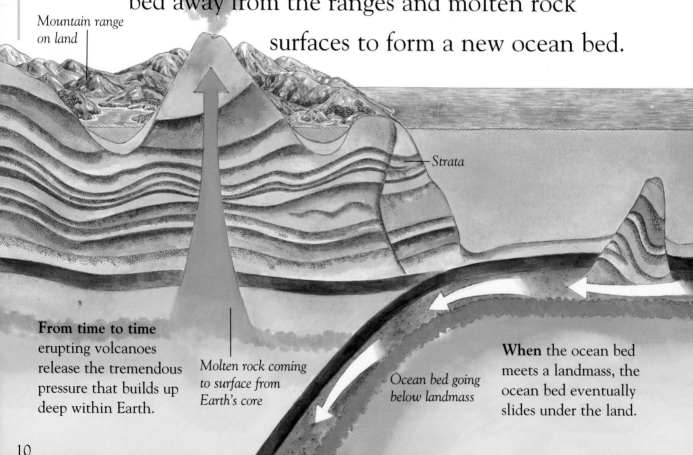

Mountain range on land

Strata

From time to time erupting volcanoes release the tremendous pressure that builds up deep within Earth.

Molten rock coming to surface from Earth's core

Ocean bed going below landmass

When the ocean bed meets a landmass, the ocean bed eventually slides under the land.

When the ocean bed meets a landmass, the pressure makes the land push upwards. The Rockies and Andes Mountains of North and South America were formed in this way.

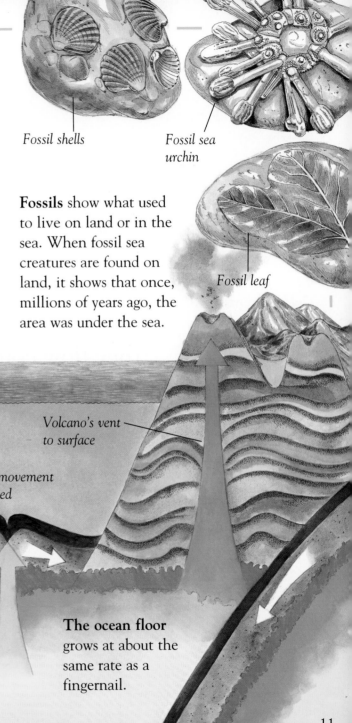

Fossil shells

Fossil sea urchin

Fossils show what used to live on land or in the sea. When fossil sea creatures are found on land, it shows that once, millions of years ago, the area was under the sea.

Fossil leaf

Volcano's vent to surface

Remains of undersea mountain

Outward movement of ocean bed

Earthquakes and active volcanoes are clues to activity at Earth's center, which is 3,956 miles (6,370 km) from the sea's surface.

The ocean floor grows at about the same rate as a fingernail.

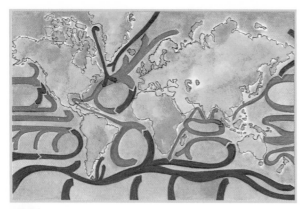

WARM CURRENTS
COLD CURRENTS

Cold currents flow from the Arctic and Antarctic Oceans toward the equator. There they absorb warmth, before returning to the polar regions.

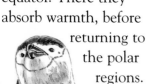

Each ocean has a system of currents. These are strong movements of water caused by Earth's rotation around the Sun. North of the equator most currents flow in a clockwise direction. South of the equator they flow counterclockwise. Tides are mostly caused by the Moon, which pulls seawater toward it and away from Earth. This causes a low tide. On the opposite side of the world there is a corresponding high tide.

Chinstrap penguins

Penguins only live in the Southern Hemisphere.

GREENLAND

NORTH
AMERICA

EUROPE

AFRICA

SOUTH
AMERICA

The cold polar
oceans are
particularly rich
in sea creatures,
from microscopic
plankton to the
huge whales that
feed on it.

Sunlight makes the sea's surface light. But this light fades as you go deeper and most sea creatures live in pitch darkness.

Seas and

oceans are very dark. Sunlight can only reach to a depth of 591 feet (180 m)—below that there is no light. But many creatures live in the ocean's darkness. Some make their own light. Others "see" by feeling changes in pressure or currents. All can withstand low temperatures because water in the ocean depths is always cold, even if it is near the equator.

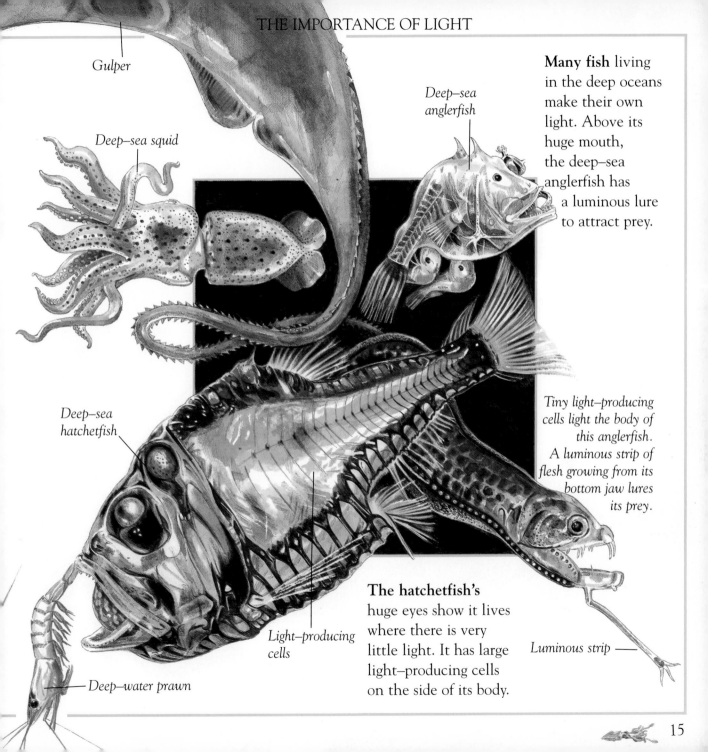

Gulper

Deep–sea squid

Deep–sea anglerfish

Many fish living in the deep oceans make their own light. Above its huge mouth, the deep–sea anglerfish has a luminous lure to attract prey.

Deep–sea hatchetfish

Tiny light–producing cells light the body of this anglerfish. A luminous strip of flesh growing from its bottom jaw lures its prey.

Light–producing cells

The hatchetfish's huge eyes show it lives where there is very little light. It has large light–producing cells on the side of its body.

Luminous strip

Deep–water prawn

15

Ganea jellyfish

Shoal of bonito

Jellyfish live in the warmer surface waters of the oceans. Their young, which are called medusae, drift near the surface.

In mid–ocean, sea temperatures change little. Differences in temperature between day and night only affect the few surface feet of water. Differences between summer and winter temperatures are felt to depths of 591 feet (180 m). Below that, the temperature hardly changes. This makes a stable environment for sea creatures.

The electric ray has special cells in its body that can give electric shocks of up to 220 volts. Although it grows to 5.9 feet (1.8 m) it only has tiny teeth. Without its electric shock system it could not kill its prey.

Electric ray

Mako shark

Squid live mainly at depths of 591 to 5,414 feet (180 to 1,650 m). They are hunted by sperm whales.

Mako shark

The blue whale can be 105 feet (32 m) long, but feeds entirely on plankton. The 13–foot (4m)–long mako shark is a swift hunter, preying on mackerel, tuna, and sardines.

Blue whale

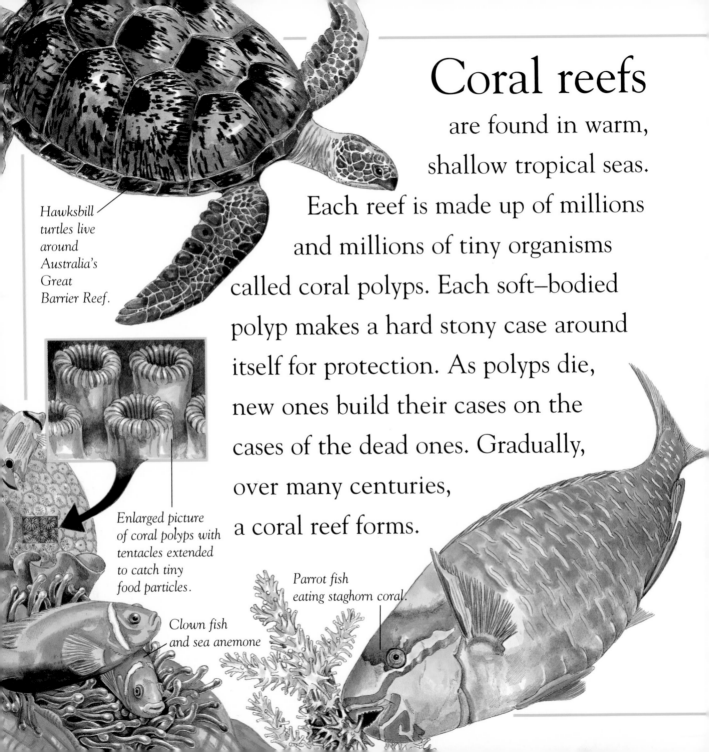

Coral reefs

are found in warm, shallow tropical seas. Each reef is made up of millions and millions of tiny organisms called coral polyps. Each soft–bodied polyp makes a hard stony case around itself for protection. As polyps die, new ones build their cases on the cases of the dead ones. Gradually, over many centuries, a coral reef forms.

Hawksbill turtles live around Australia's Great Barrier Reef.

Enlarged picture of coral polyps with tentacles extended to catch tiny food particles.

Parrot fish eating staghorn coral.

Clown fish and sea anemone

Where coral reefs are found

The pennant fish's bold stripes break up its outline, which helps protect it from predators.

The world's biggest coral reef is the Great Barrier Reef. It stretches for 1,259 miles (2,027 km) along the northeast coast of Australia.

Moray eel

Regal angelfish

Coral reefs are home to a great variety of sea creatures, from fierce moray eels to sponges and tiny, brilliantly colored fish.

Trumpet fish

Tourism threatens coral reefs. Divers touch and break the coral and clumsily dropped boat anchors smash it. But coral also has natural enemies. The crown–of–thorns starfish has destroyed parts of the Great Barrier Reef.

Crown–of–thorns starfish eating staghorn coral.

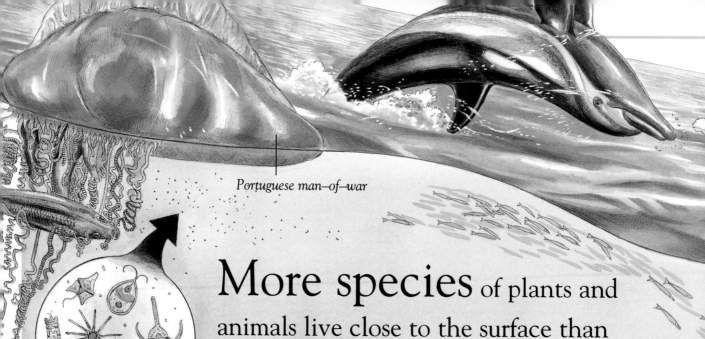

Portuguese man-of-war

Close-up of a drop of seawater

A bucket of seawater may look clear and empty, but it isn't. It will contain thousands of plants and animals too small to see without a microscope. These are the organisms that form plankton.

More species of plants and animals live close to the surface than anywhere else in the ocean. This is due to the Sun. All plants, whether they live on land or in the sea, need sunlight to make their food. So sea plants, which range from large seaweeds to microscopic diatoms, live at the surface where there is most sunlight. This means the sea animals that eat plants also live close to the surface most of the time.

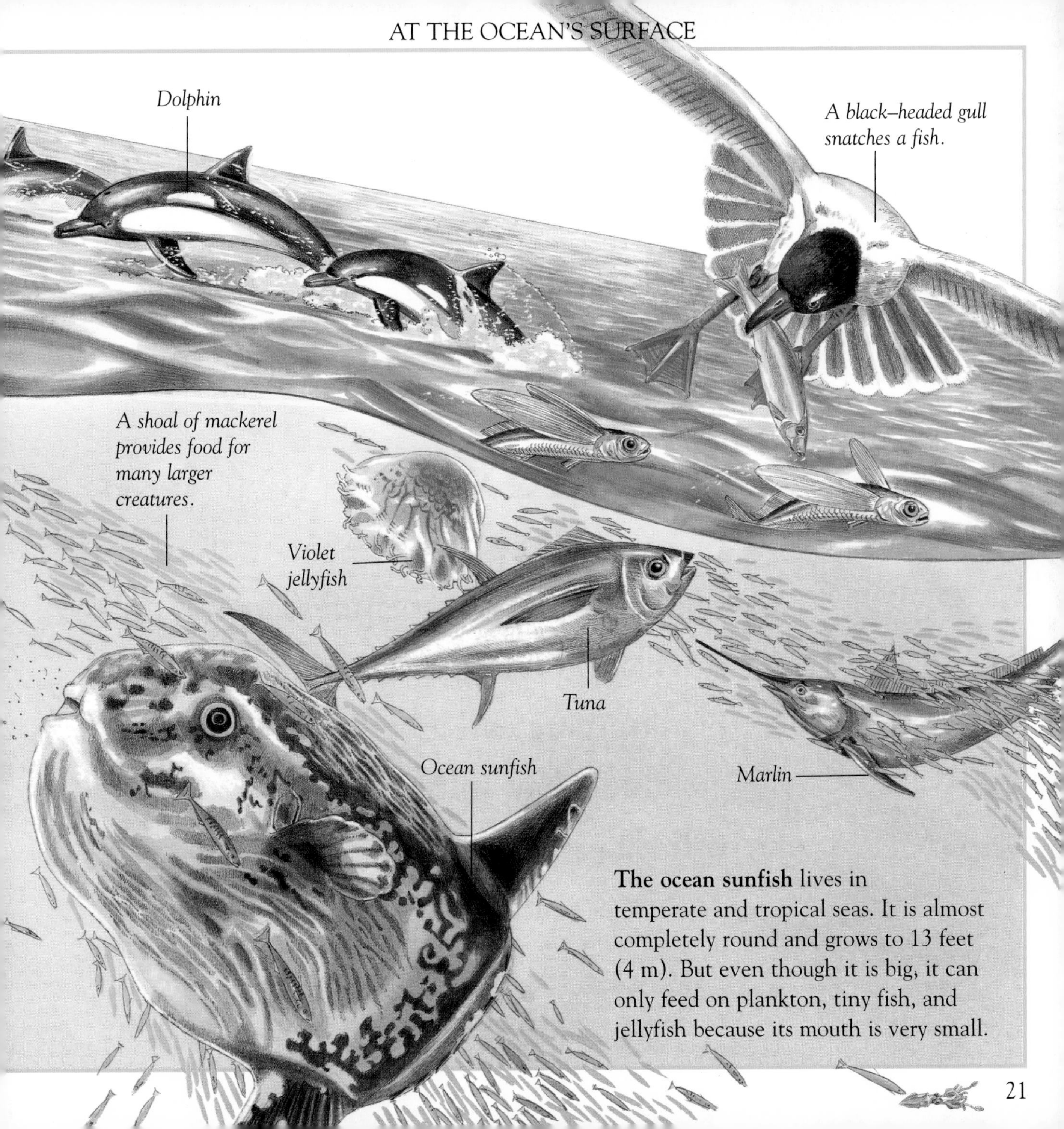

Dolphin

A black–headed gull snatches a fish.

A shoal of mackerel provides food for many larger creatures.

Violet jellyfish

Tuna

Ocean sunfish

Marlin

The ocean sunfish lives in temperate and tropical seas. It is almost completely round and grows to 13 feet (4 m). But even though it is big, it can only feed on plankton, tiny fish, and jellyfish because its mouth is very small.

21

Grey shark

Marlin

Great white shark

Baleen whale

If there were no plankton there would be no other living things in the sea. Every sea creature depends on the plankton for food. The microscopic plankton are eaten by slightly larger creatures that, in turn, are eaten by tiny fish. These are eaten by larger fish and so on, until you reach the large animals, like sharks. This is called a food chain.

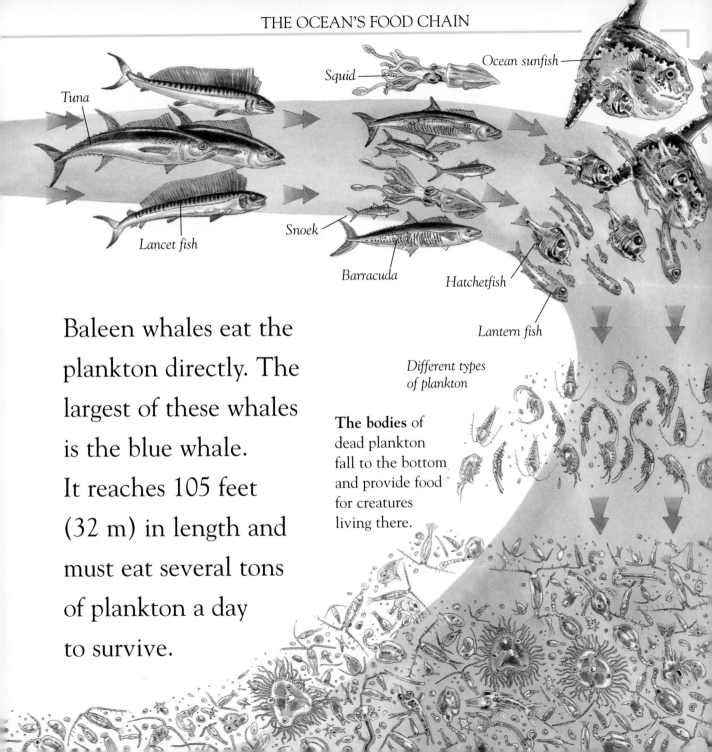

Tuna

Squid

Ocean sunfish

Lancet fish

Snoek

Barracuda

Hatchetfish

Lantern fish

Different types
of plankton

The bodies of
dead plankton
fall to the bottom
and provide food
for creatures
living there.

Baleen whales eat the plankton directly. The largest of these whales is the blue whale. It reaches 105 feet (32 m) in length and must eat several tons of plankton a day to survive.

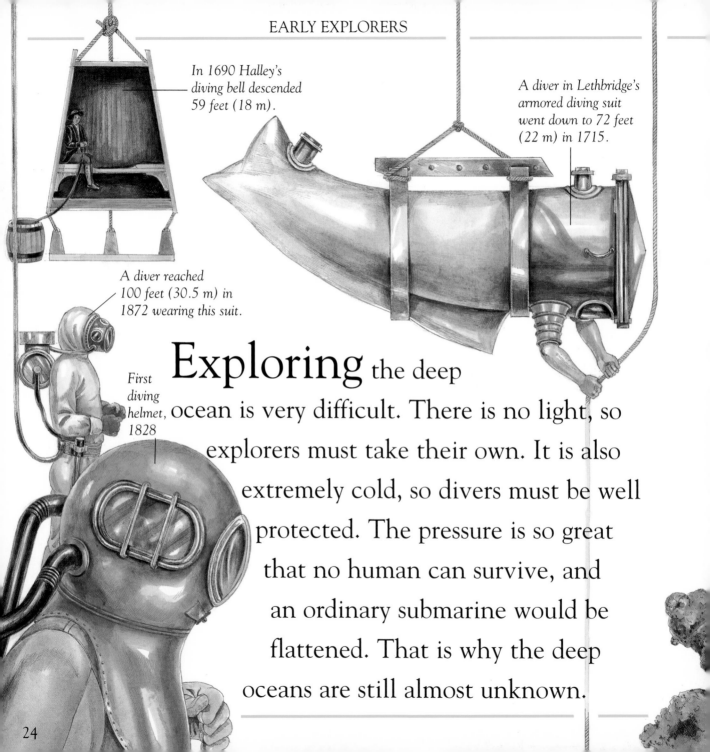

In 1690 Halley's diving bell descended 59 feet (18 m).

A diver in Lethbridge's armored diving suit went down to 72 feet (22 m) in 1715.

A diver reached 100 feet (30.5 m) in 1872 wearing this suit.

First diving helmet, 1828

Exploring the deep ocean is very difficult. There is no light, so explorers must take their own. It is also extremely cold, so divers must be well protected. The pressure is so great that no human can survive, and an ordinary submarine would be flattened. That is why the deep oceans are still almost unknown.

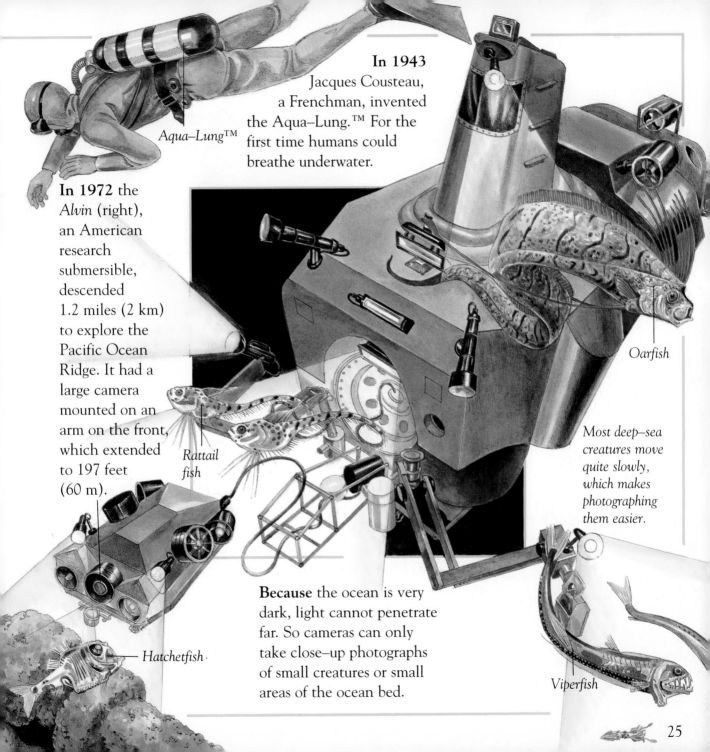

Aqua–Lung™

In 1943
Jacques Cousteau,
a Frenchman, invented
the Aqua–Lung.™ For the
first time humans could
breathe underwater.

In 1972 the
Alvin (right),
an American
research
submersible,
descended
1.2 miles (2 km)
to explore the
Pacific Ocean
Ridge. It had a
large camera
mounted on an
arm on the front,
which extended
to 197 feet
(60 m).

_Rattail
fish_

Oarfish

_Most deep–sea
creatures move
quite slowly,
which makes
photographing
them easier._

Because the ocean is very
dark, light cannot penetrate
far. So cameras can only
take close–up photographs
of small creatures or small
areas of the ocean bed.

— _Hatchetfish_ ·

Viperfish

Navigation satellite

Sailors now navigate with satellite and radio beacons. This is more accurate than relying on the Sun and the stars.

Ships beam radio waves to the nearest radio beacon. The time they take to reach the beacon is measured to find the ship's position.

Radar (**R**adio **D**etection **A**nd **R**anging) uses short radio waves to detect ships.

Cameras are positioned on the ocean bed, where they take photos at set intervals.

Today's ocean explorers still face many problems. To overcome them much exploration is done by remote control. Scientists can watch a screen and monitor information from their instruments hundreds of feet below them.

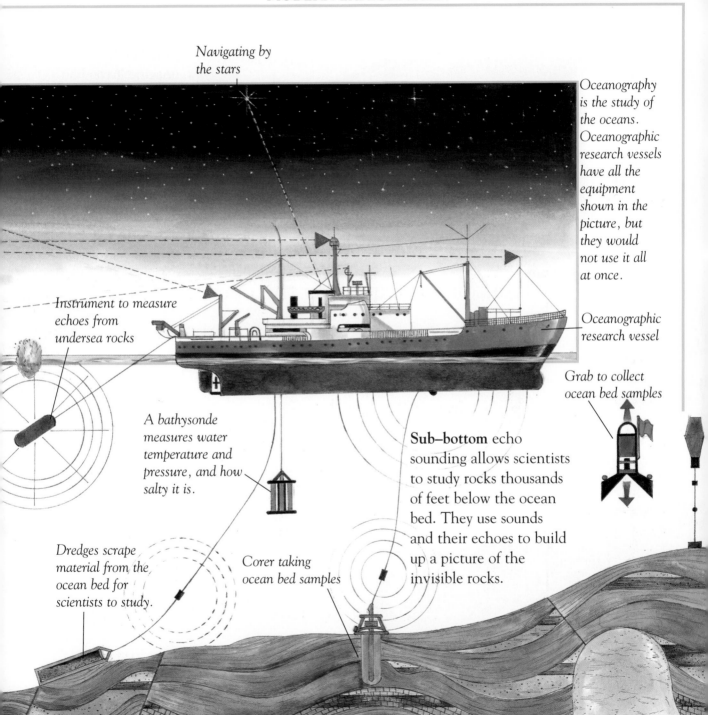

Navigating by the stars

Oceanography is the study of the oceans. Oceanographic research vessels have all the equipment shown in the picture, but they would not use it all at once.

Instrument to measure echoes from undersea rocks

Oceanographic research vessel

Grab to collect ocean bed samples

A bathysonde measures water temperature and pressure, and how salty it is.

Sub–bottom echo sounding allows scientists to study rocks thousands of feet below the ocean bed. They use sounds and their echoes to build up a picture of the invisible rocks.

Dredges scrape material from the ocean bed for scientists to study.

Corer taking ocean bed samples

Giant squid

Coelacanth

The giant squid would be hard to imagine if you had not seen it. But describing it would be very difficult!

Coelacanths survived as 90–million–year–old fossils. Then, in 1938, a live one was caught off South Africa.

Male narwhals have a long spiral tusk, just like the horn of the mythical unicorn.

Even with modern technology, exploring the oceans is difficult. So imagine what it must have been like for the first long–distance sailors in their tiny wooden boats, ocean–going canoes, or rafts. Tired, hungry, dazzled by the Sun on a calm sea, or peering through fog or the blackness of a storm, they "saw" some very strange creatures. But not all were imaginary!

Narwhal

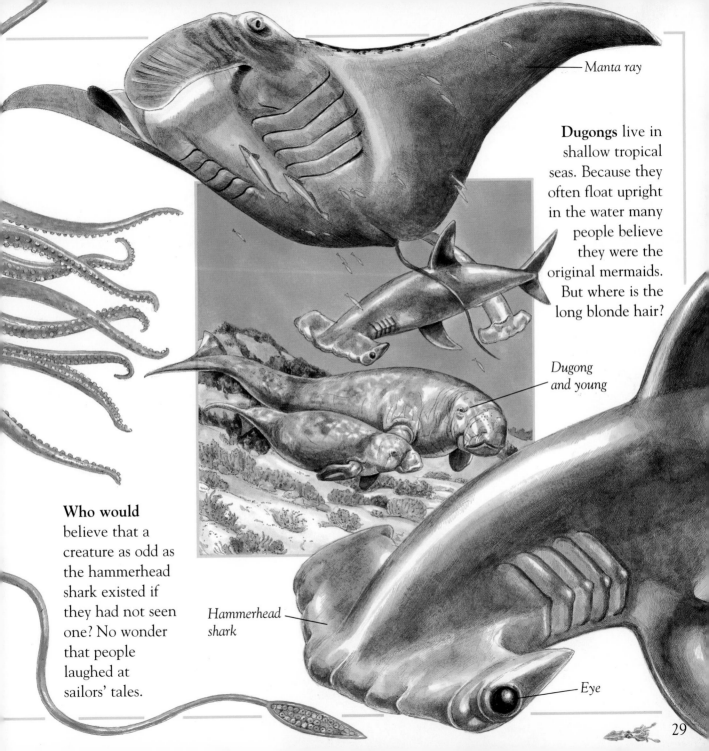

Manta ray

Dugongs live in shallow tropical seas. Because they often float upright in the water many people believe they were the original mermaids. But where is the long blonde hair?

Dugong and young

Who would believe that a creature as odd as the hammerhead shark existed if they had not seen one? No wonder that people laughed at sailors' tales.

Hammerhead shark

Eye

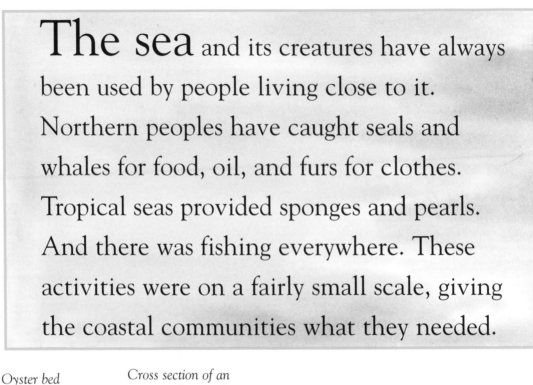

Diver

The sea and its creatures have always been used by people living close to it. Northern peoples have caught seals and whales for food, oil, and furs for clothes. Tropical seas provided sponges and pearls. And there was fishing everywhere. These activities were on a fairly small scale, giving the coastal communities what they needed.

Oyster bed

Cross section of an oyster with a pearl

If a grain of sand gets into an oyster, the oyster makes a hard covering around the sand to stop it irritating. That is how pearls are formed. In Japan the pearl divers are always women, who dive without any special equipment—they just hold their breath!

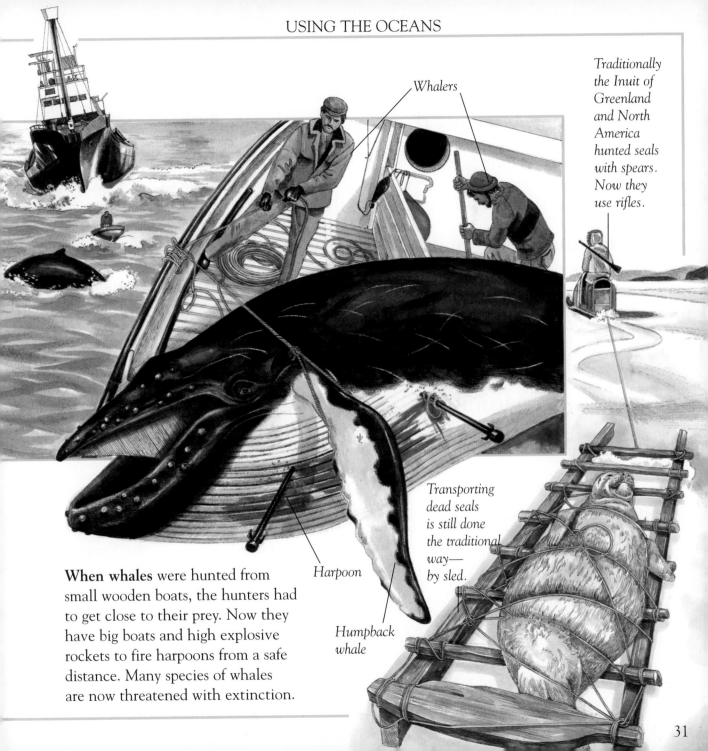

Whalers

Traditionally the Inuit of Greenland and North America hunted seals with spears. Now they use rifles.

Transporting dead seals is still done the traditional way— by sled.

Harpoon

Humpback whale

When whales were hunted from small wooden boats, the hunters had to get close to their prey. Now they have big boats and high explosive rockets to fire harpoons from a safe distance. Many species of whales are now threatened with extinction.

It is not only the waters of the seas and oceans that have many resources. In many places the bed of the deep ocean is rich in manganese, a valuable mineral. Elsewhere, oil and natural gas lie below the ocean bed. Modern technology makes it possible to extract these natural resources, but it is extremely expensive and can be very dangerous. However, we need them because our modern way of life depends on these products. But oil and gas are "fossil resources"— once they have been used up they do not form again.

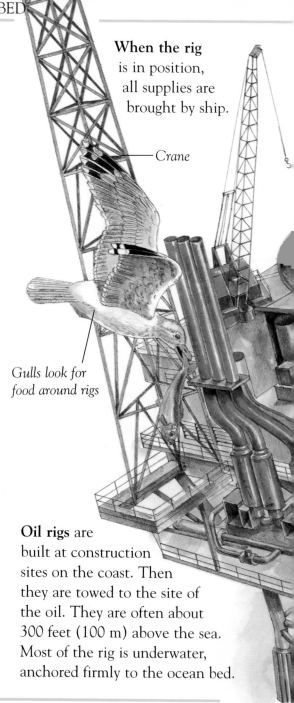

When the rig is in position, all supplies are brought by ship.

—Crane

Gulls look for food around rigs

Oil rigs are built at construction sites on the coast. Then they are towed to the site of the oil. They are often about 300 feet (100 m) above the sea. Most of the rig is underwater, anchored firmly to the ocean bed.

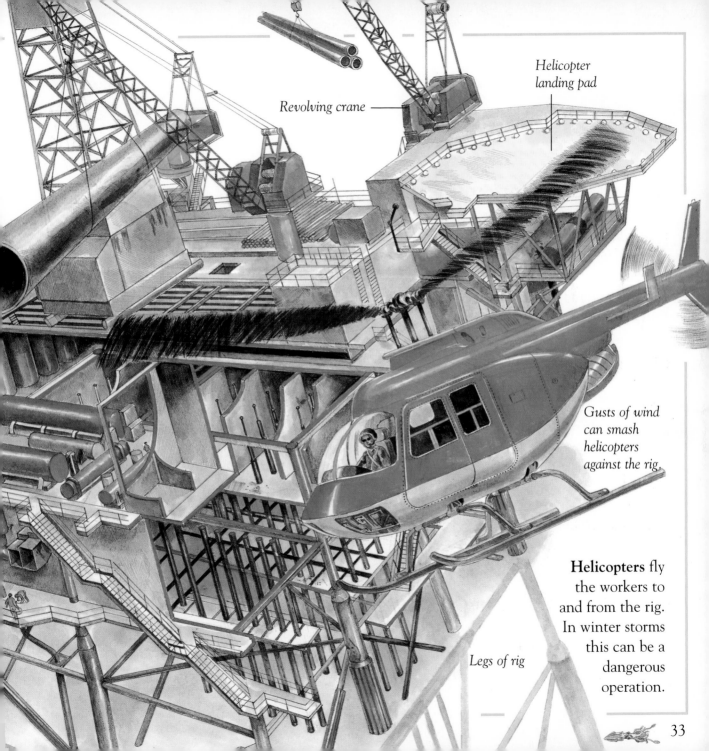

Revolving crane

Helicopter landing pad

Gusts of wind can smash helicopters against the rig.

Helicopters fly the workers to and from the rig. In winter storms this can be a dangerous operation.

Legs of rig

The smoke also causes pollution

Burning spilled oil

Oil is transported around the world in huge tankers. If one of these has an accident and spills the oil, the damage to the environment is enormous.

The world's seas and oceans are threatened, just as rain forests are on land. The increase in the world's human population means more demand for fish, oil, and natural gas. It also means more waste from humans and their factories reaching the oceans and seas. All this threatens the balance of life that has evolved in them over millions of years.

Dying seal

Shore littered with oil and rubbish

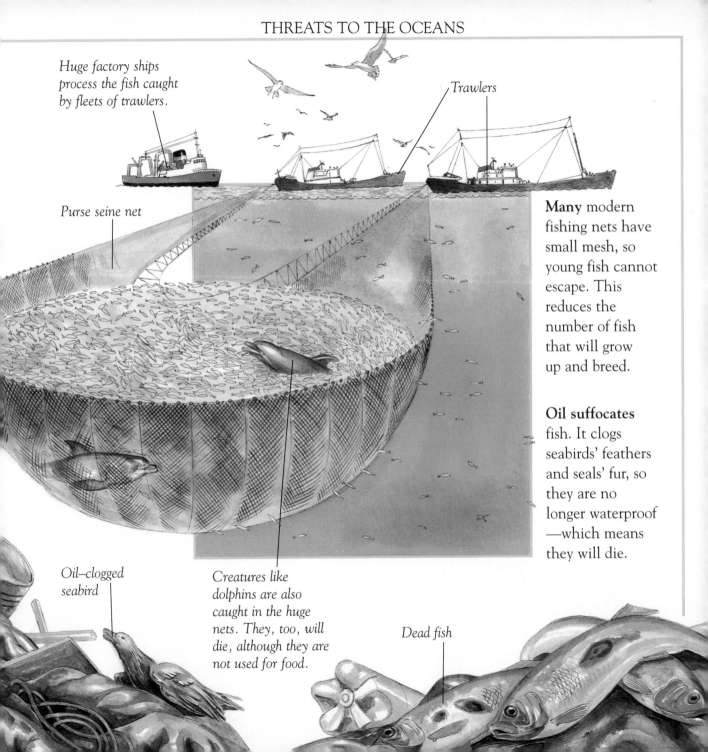

Huge factory ships process the fish caught by fleets of trawlers.

Trawlers

Purse seine net

Many modern fishing nets have small mesh, so young fish cannot escape. This reduces the number of fish that will grow up and breed.

Oil suffocates fish. It clogs seabirds' feathers and seals' fur, so they are no longer waterproof —which means they will die.

Oil–clogged seabird

Creatures like dolphins are also caught in the huge nets. They, too, will die, although they are not used for food.

Dead fish

After the Sun, the sea is the most powerful constant influence on Earth. Scientists look with wonder at the energy contained in its waves and tides. For years they have tried to find ways to use it, but with very little success.

Out in the vast space of the deep mid–ocean, tsunamis are often little bigger than normal waves.

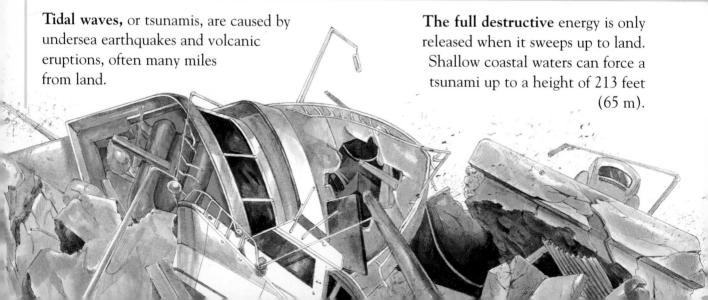

Tidal waves, or tsunamis, are caused by undersea earthquakes and volcanic eruptions, often many miles from land.

The full destructive energy is only released when it sweeps up to land. Shallow coastal waters can force a tsunami up to a height of 213 feet (65 m).

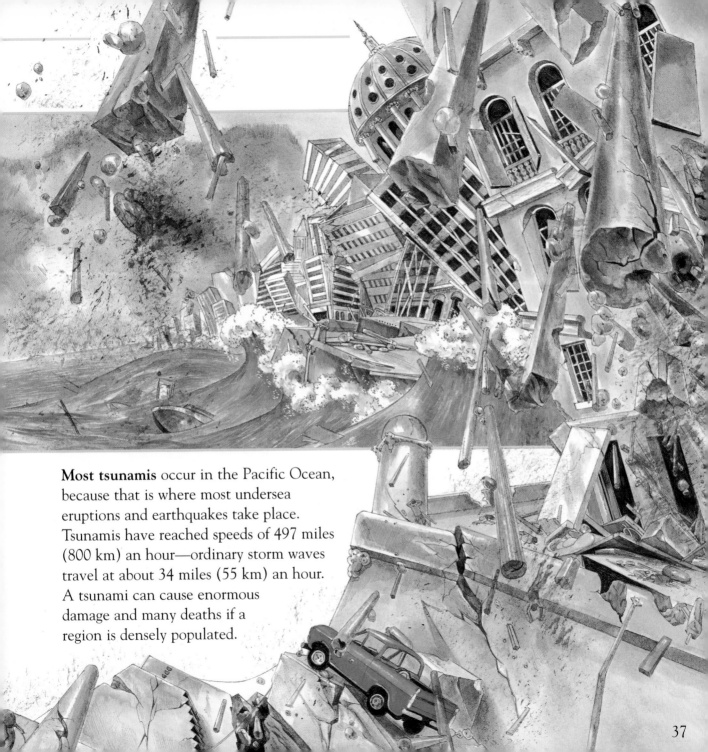

Most tsunamis occur in the Pacific Ocean, because that is where most undersea eruptions and earthquakes take place. Tsunamis have reached speeds of 497 miles (800 km) an hour—ordinary storm waves travel at about 34 miles (55 km) an hour. A tsunami can cause enormous damage and many deaths if a region is densely populated.

USEFUL WORDS

Baleen Sheets of gristly material fringed with bristles, which plankton–eating whales use to strain their food from the seawater.

Diatoms Microscopic plants found in plankton.

Extinction Any living thing on the point of being wiped out.

Hemisphere Half a sphere. The half of Earth north of the equator is the Northern Hemisphere and the half to the south is the Southern Hemisphere.

Mineral Any natural substance that has a set chemical makeup. Gold and salt are minerals, but ordinary earth is not because its chemical makeup varies.

Plankton Microscopic plants and animals that live in the seas and oceans.

Polar Cold region on land or sea near the North or South Poles.

Predator A creature that hunts for prey.

Prey A creature hunted for food.

Species Group of plants or animals that look alike, live in the same way, and produce young that do the same.

Submersible A vessel that can travel at great depths underwater.

Temperate Climate that is not very hot, very dry, very cold, or very wet. Found between tropical and polar regions.

Tropical Warm climatic region between latitudes 23° north and south of the equator.

INDEX